CW00822494

A Bitter Blood

A Bitter Blood

S. Liken

Published and printed by Lulu.com

ISBN 978-1-291-11824-7

Cover Artwork : Gareth Morton

Contact : stuliken@hotmail.co.uk

<u>Acknowledgements and Thanks</u>

To my wife and daughters for their inspiration

To Warrington Poetry Group for encouragement and advice

Special thanks to P.J. Kimber and Gareth Morton for advanced layout consideration

Contents

50. Puppy

51. Assistant

52. Circus

53. Ghosts

54. Executed

55. Inside

56. People

57. Gorilla

58. Dad

59. Holidays

60. Kidnappers

61. Adore

62. Rebels

63. Nightmare

64. Clown

65. Sneaky

66. Business

67. Michelangelo

68. Elephant

69. Moaning

70. Stanley

71. Poor

72. Yacht Race

73. Demons

74. Test

75. S & M

76. Wonder Woman

77. Zombie

78. Mary

79. Bargain

80. Hands

81. Tea

82. Zoo

83. Cannibals

84. Houdini

85. Frankenstein

A Bitter Blood

A Modern (Grown Up) Nursery Rhyme

Monday's child has pierced her face

Tuesday's child is a swearing disgrace

Wednesday's child is dyslexic and slow

Thursday's child has got an ASBO

Friday's child is shoving, not giving

Saturday's child signs on for a living

And the child that Britney had last Sunday

Will probably drink Meths, take drugs and turn gay….

Accidental death

She polished the floor
At the top of the stairs
Sawed halfway through
The legs of the chairs...
Poured cold water
On the icy path
Switched on a heater
Right next to the bath...
Turned all the sharp knives
Around in the drawers
Removed the safety guards
From my rotating saws...
Loosened the glass
Round each mirror's edge
Lit all the candles
On the narrowest ledge...
Took out the screws
On the banister's rails
Tilted the pictures
Exposing the nails...
Opened the rat poison
From under the sink
Next to the bottles
Of milk that I drink...
She sharpened the lid
On the big first aid box
Scattered razor blades
In the drawer for my socks...
Moved the fire extinguisher
Near the cooker's hot rings
Exposed the bare flex
On all electrical things...

She rinsed each apple,
Pear, orange and peach
With drain cleaner,
Dishwasher fluid and bleach...
Took the fuse out of the toaster
And bent back the wire
And did something dodgy
To the living room fire...
She pulled up the tacks
To make the stair carpet loose
The whole house is a death trap
There is no excuse...
For the stunts that she's pulled
Like the paraffin heater
Next to the bag
Of charcoal and saltpetre...
Then there are the switches
That give off a wild spark
Or the radio-active stuff
That glows in the dark...
There is no insurance
To be paid if I die
So the serious question
I must ask is "why?..."
What did I do lately
To cause so much distress?
All I said was...
Her bum...
Looked ...
Quite big...
In...
that dress!!

Adios

Dear Sir, here's a letter
I've tried many times to write
I've been at it all the weekend
And I've stayed up half the night
It concerns our recent trip
To your little hotel in Spain
I'm sorry to have to tell you
We won't be coming back again
At first when we got there
Just landed from the plane
We thought "this looks quite lovely
And we really can't complain"
But fourteen days later
I think we've changed our mind
Please don't think us ungrateful
Or beastly, or unkind
But when you hear our stories
About what happened in your land
You may even have to agree with us
Or at least try to understand
And when you reach the conclusion
Of my sad and touching letter
I hope your opinion of us might change
A little – for the better
Okay now that you're wondering
What made us so irate
It wasn't the 'English Bastards' sign
Hanging from your gate
It wasn't your miserable concierge
Drunk and passed out on the floor
Or your stupid lift attendant
Was he really your brother in law?
It wasn't the noisy handymen
Playing footie in the corridors
Or the gardener cum businessman
Trying to interest me in whores

It wasn't the way your cleaners
Sneered and snarled and stole
It wasn't the fact they didn't leave
A solitary toilet roll
It wasn't the sound of vacuums
At six thirty in the halls
Or the anti British graffiti
That they daubed upon the walls
It wasn't the dirty tableware
Or cockroaches that we hate
Or the flies that swarmed around our food
On each dirty glass and plate
It wasn't the phones that didn't work
Or the shower stall full of mud
Or the permanently blocked toilets
Or the bidet filled with blood
It wasn't the missing holiday rep
When our luggage disappeared
It wasn't the one armed driver
Though I admit - he was quite weird
It wasn't your lack of understanding
Of how much we were in trouble
It wasn't the service tax on the bill
Or the way you charged us double
It wasn't the day that woman went mad
And threatened me with a knife
I wouldn't have punched her quite so hard
If I'd known she was your wife
It wasn't my children crying
Or my wife's kidnapping in your town
It wasn't my fifth electrocution
Or my predictable breakdown
Our only complaint about your hotel
And the way that it was run...
Is for two whole weeks in August
What happened to the Sun?

Bad Luck

Over the Christmas holidays
I had a touch of flu
This turned into pneumonia
That's when I thought of you…

Remember when you said to me
Things could always be worse
I recalled those fateful words
And it made me swear and curse…

My car's exploded and blown a seal
And it's going to cost a bomb
My job has just been terminated
Where's the cash going to come from?

My fridge defrosts whenever it wants
My telly is on the blink
The microwave has taken up smoking
And my wife has turned to drink…

My kids have holes in their clothes and shoes
The goldfish is floating in his tank
The cat's left home, the dog has died
And we get death threats from the bank…

Mum died leaving massive debts
One spoon, one plate, one cup
And if the undertaker isn't paid
They said they'll dig her up!

The garden's full of poisonous weeds
My fence collapsed into the street
Next door's dog dumped his breakfast too
So watch where you put your feet…

The roof's missing tiles, the chimney's gone
The gutter's falling down
The electric's going haywire
And my bath water's a dirty brown…

I'm on tablets for stress relief
Since the bailiffs took my settee
And if they come back for my ceramic pot
I won't have anywhere to pee…

An eviction notice has just arrived
My landlord's so unfeeling
The windows are cracked, it's freezing cold
When the rain drips through the ceiling…

My three piece suite's now an orange box
With two cartons left and right
The coffee table's an upturned pail
And my wallpaper fell off last night…

This is the end, I've had enough
It's depression that really kills
But the aspirin bottle's got a child proof cap
And I can't get out the pills!

The cupboard's bare, the food is gone
No tins of beans of spam or stew
We've just shared a jar of Marmite
From nineteen ninety two…

We're hallucinating from hunger
The wife's looking like a joint of pork
One of my kids has got a knife
The other one's got a fork…

I'm keeping warm by burning bills
And final demands outlined in red
I'm cold from six of us sharing one duvet
And three of them wetting the bed!

So next time you think you're helping
When you make comments on my health
And say that things could even be worse
Just go and… Physician, heal thyself!

Blind Date

My new job moved me miles away
From my relatives and friends
So I needed a fresh social life
Like my self help book recommends
So I joined a dating agency
And paid them their large fee
Then answered all the questions
About what type of girls for me
I thought I wanted one with beauty
And one who's really smart
Or one who's kind and thoughtful
Or likes poetry and art
I might prefer a sporty type
Who loves training in the gym
Or one who likes to slalom ski
Or run or jog or swim
Finally the dating computer stopped
And found my perfect mate
It even booked the restaurant
And arranged times with my date
The next seven days that followed
Made me feel quite scared
Since all I did was worry
Was I well enough prepared?
Saturday couldn't come too soon
As I practiced things to say
And ninety things to talk about
Between the starter and sorbet
Then other factors start to appear
And infiltrate my thoughts
Like should I order for us in French?
And should I dress in shorts?
Then, what if she prefers taller men
Or ones who wear sharp suits
What if she likes men in checkered shirts
With jeans and cowboy boots?
Or what if she prefers the biker type
With long hair, and jacket made of leather
(I've got a camel hair overcoat
That suits the British weather)

What about a shaven head
Or a muscly kind of guy
Or one with tattoos all over his arms
Or a pirate, with one eye?
I worried about the date so much
I almost cancelled twice
But my self help book said be positive
And it might turn out rather nice
Throwing caution to the wind
I reached the bistro's door
And looked around to try to see
What I'd let myself in for…
The next thirty seconds
I would rather not relate
As that computer must have hiccupped
When it sent us on this date
Let's just say within that moment
We knew things weren't quite right
No way were we compatible
She was such an awful sight
And I'd stated that the age range
Should be twenty to thirty three
But the woman wearing the carnation
Was more than twice as old as me
Her hair was grey, her teeth were false
Her wooden leg was weird
Her broken nose was badly set
And she showed just a hint of beard
The only thing we agreed on
Was that the computer must have lied
When it came to matching her with me
All our expectations truly died
We did agree to meet again
To demand our fees returned
And we'd put this down to experience
And a lesson harshly learned
There is another footnote
To the situation that I'm in
I got that stupid self help book
And dumped it in the bin!

Bravery

I've never fought a fiery dragon
Or braved four men at noon
Never crossed the sea in a boat
Or joined Armstrong on the moon

Never rescued cats from trees
Or dealt with raging forest fires
Never lifted up a truck to save
A child beneath its tyres

Never fought with savage wolves
Or tackled terrorists in mid-air
Never brought a puppy out from a well
Or wrestled a panther in its lair

Never faced a vicious gang
Or a maniac who's fought with the law
Never breathed life into a drowning man
Who was washed up on the shore

I've never done anything that heroic
All these things are true
But I'm still the bravest man alive ...
I went and married you!

Chocolate (can be bad for you)

In the off licence one Friday evening
I hear what sounds like a fight
All I wanted was a small bar of chocolate
But what happened next ruined my night…

The owner comes crashing through the cornflakes
He's got hold of some lad by the shirt
They're punching and gouging and biting
It's likely that someone'll get hurt…

I'm waiting to pay for my chocolate
Ignoring the fight on the floor
The owner's hit the lad's head on the counter
Quite casual – like he's done it before…

The lad comes back with an uppercut
And hits the bloke's chin once or twice
I'm considering coming back in the morning
Because bashed tins are usually half price…

The owner's wife is panicked and screaming
Then she's grabbed the cash tray from the till
From out the back she's shouted a warning
"I've already rung the Old Bill!"

I've slammed my cash down on the counter
This situation's made me irate
I've been stood there politely and quiet
I don't see why I ought to wait…

So to get past the fighters I struggle
Wanting just to go out through the door
When I get a sudden truncheon in the goolies
Wielded by the full force of the law…

Six strapping great beefy policemen
Were then attacked by the back of my head
I smudged their boots so beautifully polished
And left their knuckles so raw and so red…

I got arrested for aggravated bruising
And bleeding without due care and attention
I could elaborate more on my injuries
But they were really too numerous to mention…

The owner in the cop shop was rubbish
He must have had too many blows to the head
When they put me and the lad in a lineup
The idiot picked me out instead!

Up in front of the Magistrates
I tried in vain to argue my case
But it's hard to go into much detail
With boot marks all over one's face!

So for the sake of a small bar of chocolate
I got well fitted up by the law
And to go nicely along with my bruises
Now I eat all my meals through a straw!

So the moral to this cautionary tale
If you're in the wrong place and time
Make sure there's some other poor scapegoat
Around to take the blame for your crime!

Just one final and important postscript
There's one off licence less now in town
No one knew how the fires got started
But the police station also burned down…..

Confusion

My washing machine's broken
The dishwasher's also kaput
The microwave's acting so weirdly
And the fridge door's just fell on my foot!

I'm not too good with appliances
There's water all over the floor
There's smoke coming out of the oven
I don't think I can handle much more.

The kettle is sparking like crazy
The toaster has burnt all the bread
This kitchen is trying to kill me
I think I might eat out instead.

The dryer has chewed up my trousers
The mixer's come on by itself
The freezer has iced up the windows
The blender's blown up on the shelf.

Ever since we had trouble with electrics
There's just nothing left I can use
I knew I should not have suggested
The wife repairs her own blinking fuse!

Cut Price Superhero

I'm a cut price superhero
Because the people in this town
Will only pay for ten hours a week...
(They're trying to keep the costs down)

I'm a sort of Semi – Hulk
Now that guy really is strong
I can lift cars above my head...
(But not for all that long)

Spiderman swings from wall to wall
In his suit of bright blue and red
I suppose I could swoop from a giant web too...
(But I prefer escalators instead)

Superman has got x-ray vision
And can see through walls with his sight
I get two for one at Specsavers now...
(So I'm ok till about nine at night)

Some heroes have fortresses deep underground
Others hide in caves like a bat
The rich ones often own a building or two
(Cut price hero has a shared council flat)

Batman leaps high and soars in the air
In a close simulation of flying
I'd do the same if I really had to...
(But only if people were dying)

Iron Man is clad in a bright metal suit
Others hide behind masks made of leather
I've got a hat, a scarf, boots and a cape...
(But my costume depends on the weather)

So when the world is finally saved
And all the villains are under control
I'll go back to what I was doing before...
(Signing on, every week, on the dole)

D.I.V.O.R.C.E

Last night the wife approached me
With "that look" upon her face
I got quite excited
And my heart began to race
She said "there's an announcement
That I need to make to you
I'd be interested in your reply
And to hear your point of view
I think that we should separate
For reasons I'll list now
And when you've heard the things I've said
We can have a little row
The first thing I must tell you
Is that I no longer care
And with all the lads on your football team
I'm having an affair
And whilst we're on the subject
Of the sports and things you do
I've been seeing some of the chaps
In the karate dojo you go to
There are all your pals in the weightlifting team
With their muscles big and strong
And on the days I'm feeling horny
I make them bring their friends along
Your Rugby mates are all quite fit
And I see them every week
You're probably quite shocked at this
And you might think I'm a freak
It's not really about the sex
Though I must admit that's great
It's the fact that I can still make you beg
And you always have to wait"
At these words I must admit
I felt quite humiliated
So I calmed myself with a cup of tea
Until my anger had abated

The brief pause in her soliloquy
Allowed me chance to reply
So I held her lightly by the shoulders
And I looked her in the eye
Then I said in a quite calm voice
"My Dear, you're probably right
When I think of all the times we've spent
In arguments every night
But whilst we're talking like Adults
For you - here's a little treat
What I'm about to say might upset you
So why don't you take a seat?
Remember your cousin's wedding
When the rain kept us all inside
Well that day I did all nine bridesmaids
And I even had the bride
And as for the girls in your aerobics class
I know each one intimately
And I've fettled the entire knitting club
That you invite round for their tea
Your library group and your swimming team
Your step class and the girls who do your hair
And every single baby sitter
Even the one's I couldn't bear
For every one of my friends you've had
I've had three or four of yours
And that's not including female relatives
Or the prostitutes and whores
It's amazing what Viagra can do
When your partner's a proven cheat
I've heard everything about you
From every woman in our street
So my revenge is rather sweet
When you hear my harsh reply
I think I've given you an STD
And there's a chance that you might die!"

Dear Son

Dear son here's a message
That we're leaving just for you
It may explain in a bit more detail
Just what we're about to do…

Want to tell you up front
We think you're a real great guy
But there are one or two things lately
That have really caught our eye…

Under your bed there's an ancient pizza
And a half full tin of beans
An assortment of dubious underwear
And those girlie magazines…

Now you know we don't like to complain
About things you choose to hide
But the smell from that cornucopia
Resembles something that's just died…

The bathroom isn't much better
In fact the smells in there are foul
We're not even going to ask you
What you've wiped upon that towel…

Can I also point out the places
Where you don't leave your football kit
Especially muddy boots or jerseys
Where people need to sit…

And while we're on the subject
About leaving stuff here and there
Could you please give back my tweezers
Without all your nostril hair?

And your TV and your stereo system
Of which we know you're really proud
At three thirty in the morning
Must they be so blinking loud?

And since we're on the subject
About things we object to
There's your poor choice of companions
Who behave as badly as you do…

So when you come in from college
And you say we're the parents from hell
Could we just politely mention
Our home isn't your hotel…

So apart from all the untidiness
And the awful things we often see
Combined with the smells and bad behaviour
Or your unhygienic proclivity…

Here's something that you should know
Now you're really in the mire
Your dinner will be really burnt
'Cos the chip shop caught on fire…

And as for all the washing and ironing
That you imagine comes from heaven
The launderette is open weekdays
From eight thirty until seven…

And finally to let you know how much
You've driven us to despair
Your father and I are moving house
But we're not going to tell you where!!!!

Descendant of Daedalus

Southwest of the island of Samos
Lies the deadly Icarian Sea
Named after a famous Greek story
About a lad trying to reach Sicily.
Now this lad had a real famous father
He built the labyrinth in Crete for the King
But he made a false cow for the Queen there
Where she, and a bull, had a fling.
The result of this fling was the Minotaur
And this made King Minos quite mad
So he threw poor old Daedalus in prison
Then decided to chuck in his lad.
Now Daedalus, as I said, was quite clever
So he sat down and thought "What a cheat!
I built the old king that fine Labyrinth
Then he sticks me in jail, here in Crete!"
So up to his young son went Daedalus
And said "Icarus, come here, heed my words,
Go and fetch me some great big wax candles
And those feathers you collect off the birds."
But Icarus wasn't as smart as his father
And just liked staring up at the sky
Which eventually proved his undoing
Watching all of those birds flying high.
So those wings that poor Daedalus had created
And arranged with such care on their backs
Went and melted as daft lad got careless
And his feathers ran right out of wax.
If only he'd listened to Daedalus
And not thought to fly off and have fun
Thinking he could soar like an Osprey
Then getting too close to the sun.
So the boy who felt just like an Eagle
As he fell to his death in the sea
Had a thought flash right through his brain then
"They might name this place after me!"
Poor Daedalus his Dad was heartbroken
When his son crashed down, and was dying
He looked up from his much lower flight path
And said "what a terrible example of flying!"
Now when the Greeks tell the myth of poor Icarus
There's a warning in the story they wrote
By all means come and visit the Cretans
But be sure that you get there by boat!

Devilishly Handsome

Not having had much success with girls
I decided to do something extreme
So I called up the Devil on an old Ouija board
And asked him to consider my scheme.

He said "Prove to me how desperate you are,
And how much do you want to succeed?
To be attractive to the opposite sex
Will you give up your soul for your need?"

He said "In a few years when your lust has calmed down
And your libido has probably diminished
Don't forget that your soul will still be just mine
And your connection to God will have finished!"

I said "I don't care; I just need to meet girls
Can I have one that looks like Bardot?"
The Devil looked sly, then said with a grin
"I could dig up that Marilyn Monroe!"

Now years have gone by, since my meeting with Nick
I'm still no luckier with any female
I suppose that the boils on my skin aren't much help
Or the horns, or the hooves or the tail.

I saw in the mirror, the last time I dared look
That I seem to have rotted away
And that sneaky Devil has still got my soul
So my new body looks likely to stay.

I'm not going to complain about my self induced fate
I won't moan or grumble or cry
I'll just lie in my pit and keep biding my time
And wait for Shakira to die!

Duck!

Took little'un to visit ducks on t' duck pond
But not one single canard did we see
That's because it had just finished spitting
They were all huddled beneath a big tree
Me and little'un had brought some bread wi' us
And we thought they'd think it were grand
When we crouched under tree to give it to 'em
And us with a loaf in each hand
But the ducks were having none of it
In a panic a few started to flap
They took off into t' sky rather rapid
And one left a hint on me cap
Happen those ducks were deliberately nasty
Or a particular horrible breed
I wondered if it were bread that they hated
Or just had a preference for seed
I thought of shouting out something horrid
That'd make 'em fly South, or off course
So I told little'un to yell something nasty
She came up with the words "Orange Sauce"
Just one further thing I should mention
The child shouted the word "duck" to me
For once I just thought to ignore her
And walked straight into t'branch of yon tree
Now I'm probably not best one to say it
As I'm usually a man of few words
But those ducks were so downright obnoxious
They reet put me off keeping birds
So as little'un were going off homeward
A long trail of crumbs leading back
I grabbed a handful of blackberries for supper
And a nice juicy duck in me sack...

Fiendishly Clever

I once ran an antique shop
And one day found a book
Covered in dust and cobwebs
But it was worth a second look
I read the title that's embossed
On the cover and the spine
I opened it quite carefully
And jumped at its first line
It said "You've just opened me
On the sixth day of June
At six oh six precisely
And invoked a mystic rune
The content of these pages
Contain an ancient spell
But if not used correctly
Will consign your soul to Hell"
Now normally my reading
Might stop at Byron, Keats or Shelley
But I know a bit about scary stuff
Cause I've seen it on the telly
Frankenstein, the Werewolf
Or the monster with no face
None of that really scares me
I prefer films set in outer space
So I simply put the book back
And then switched off the light
Locked the shop, got on my bike
And cycled home that night
But as I was getting into bed
A Demon suddenly appeared
He was perched just where the wife sits
So I thought "that's really weird
Normally she's got curlers in
And a mud pack upon her face"
But he looked even stranger
As he sat there in her place
His chin was resting on his hand
And his brow was heavy set

He looked at me quite curiously
Then said "We've never met
But I'm the Demon from your book
That you invoked tonight
So if you don't want to rot in Hell
You and I must fight...
It won't be what you're expecting
With swords or "hand to hand"
It'll be a battle of wits instead
But you must understand
If I win I get to keep
Your immortal soul from now
But you can choose whatever you wish
Should you succeed somehow"
I thought "fair enough, I'll have a go
I'll put him to the test.
Then maybe once this Demon's gone
I'll get a bit of rest!"
He said "I've travelled through the Universe
And every place you know, I've seen
So your first task is to send me
Somewhere that I've never been"
I pondered for a moment
And with my fingers crossed
I said those words that beat him
Simply this - "GET LOST"
Of course that was something
That he really couldn't handle
So he disappeared in a burst of fire
Like a miniature Roman Candle
And now I've got a brand new shop
In an exclusive London street
Cause that Demon wasn't clever
And not too difficult to beat
And as for the wife, I swapped her
For a girl who's seventeen
Since I no longer deal in antique books
Just gentlemen's magazines....

Free Telephone Help

Here at the Bureau of Mental Health
We've set up a telephone line
So follow the simple instructions
To get the help that you need, in no time.
To all you Obsessive Compulsives
We know that you would never complain
So if you've got OCD quite badly
Press ONE, then again, then again, then again.
If you are Nervous and Worried
All you must do is press TWO
But if you're a Needy, Reliant Co-Dependant
Then get someone to press TWO for you.
Now we know some customers are Delusional
So for you, please press number THREE
This will connect you to Alpha Centauri
Or the mother ship that came back for E.T.
FOUR is for Multiple Personalities
With a crisis of identity in their head
So if we ring back and ask for Napoleon
We'll expect to get Jesus or Gandhi instead.
Should you suffer from Acute Paranoia
Just hold down the button marked FIVE
Then the people who've being trying to kill you
Will know that you're still around and alive.
Please push 666 to talk to the Devil
If you're Confused, and in a state of Distress
But if you have Manifested Schizophrenia
Then the voices will say next what to press.
SEVEN is the number for Manic Depressives
If you're feeling quite lost and alone
After twenty minutes you may as well hang up
No one's coming to answer the phone.
Those of you with Bipolar Disorder
And find yourself too impatient to wait
Should press the hash key and star key repeatedly
Then change your mind and suddenly press EIGHT.
If you have Post Trauma Disorder and Dyslexia
With Work Related Stress, please press NINE
Then sob quietly to yourself whilst you're waiting
For our Operators to connect to your line.
But if you have followed all these instructions
And these alternatives aren't the answers you seek
Have a lie down and take two or three aspirins
Then ring back at the same time next week!

I've Lost Her

In the shop when they passed by
A tear they noticed in my eye
The shop girls couldn't help but stare
As so forlornly I stood there
"Are you ok, love?" they gently said
"It looks as though someone is dead"
"I've lost the wife, and furthermore
I think this was her favourite store
And this tin I hold, how much it means
These were her favourite type of beans"
"Oh you poor man" said shop girl One
"How sad it is your wife has gone"
And then, so strange to a man like me
She planted kisses one, two, three…
Not to be beaten, girl number Two
Wrapped her arms round me like glue
And hugged me close with all her might
I could have stayed like that all night…
Girl One, not wanting to be outdone
Massaged my shoulders and tried to run
Her hands softly down my back
I almost had a heart attack!
Girl Two, whose name was Serb or Czech
Fluttered eyelashes on my neck
And kissed me softly on the cheek
The best fun that I'd had all week
'You poor, poor dear' both girls then said
'It's awful to think your wife is dead
And now you're left here all alone
So sad if all your family's grown
And moved away to pastures new
Is there anything that we might do
To help you take your pain away?'
I could have hugged and kissed all day
Then suddenly, just as I feared
The wife magically reappeared

And said "this time you've gone too far
Take the shopping, get in the car
And don't try stunts like that no more
Or your next meals are through a straw!
And as for you two gullible fools
My husband don't play by the rules
And his sob story never fails
He's had girls before with his tall tales
That's the last time his eye will roam
Just wait till I get the ratbag home!
He'll be filled with such remorse
When I surprise him with divorce
I'll make him cry, the evil louse
When bailiffs come and take his house
Just wait, you'll see him really sob
When he's doing twice the hours at his job
To pay for all the things I need
Miss his wife? He will indeed!"
The girls looked at the wife once more
And walked her calmly to the door
Then glancing quickly over my way
I heard one girl softly say
'The poor man, how he'll want to cry
No wonder he had a tear in each sad eye
What a cow, a bitch, a shrew
What a witch he's married to!'
Just then the manager appeared
And said, "Girls, that was rather weird
That couple that went out the door
I think I've seen them here before
Last time, when they staged a fight
I lost a trolley full that night
Did he say that his wife was dead?
I think he's playing with your head
She steals shopping, he pretends she's died
Well, her name's Bonnie, and his name's Clyde."

Monty's Bird

I want to return this dead parrot
That I bought from this very boutique
I didn't notice he was actually a goner
When I purchased him here just last week.
I wanted a bird to be proud of
I wanted a pet to be prized
I wanted to show off to my cronies
But I can't if he's bleeding demised.
I know Norwegian blues can be sleepy
And boy, do those birds like a nap
But the only time I've seen any movement
Was when you gave the cage a wee tap.
If I'd known he was pushing up the daisies
I wouldn't have spent the cash that I did
I could have bought a filigree Siberian hamster
With my disposable fifty five quid.
If I'd realised he was past it
I wouldn't have taken him back home with me
It's no good buying exotic ex-flyers
No matter how beautiful their plumage might be.
Don't try and tell me he's resting
Don't say they like kipping on their backs
If you hadn't nailed him down in the first place
I'd have noticed some movement he lacks.
He's not stunned he's not resting in a deep sleep
He's not singing or whistling any chords
His eyes aren't even frigging open
And he's not pining for the bloody Fjords!
He's died and gone to meet his maker
This poor bird has now ceased to be
I'll report you to the pet shop association
If I don't get a replacement imme - diately.
He's run down the curtain and expired
Bereft of life he now rests in peace
So do something about my erstwhile Polly
Seeing as he is recently deceased.
I know returning my payment is awkward
And some might just question your decision
To provide me with reimbursement…
But I didn't expect the Spanish Inquisition!

Next Door

There's a shopping trolley in the garden
And a car that's up on bricks
The fence is virtually in pieces
It's impossible to fix
The wall is crumbling and decayed
The guttering's a mess
The garden's overgrown with weeds
It's a jungle - more or less
The kids are so obnoxious
No more horrid could you find
Their language is appalling
Their behaviour's unrefined
The oldest girl's a junkie
And a dirty stinking whore
Her twin brother's a delinquent
And is wanted by the law
The younger ones are drinkers
And there are needles at their feet
Their drain's blocked with used condoms
They throw their empties in the street
The mother is repulsive
Everything about her is unclean
If you said shampoo or soap to her
She wouldn't know quite what you mean
The father's never worked in years
They claim benefits galore
And every social service plan
Seems to pay them more and more
They're the heroes of the underclass
With their grasping, thieving attitude

They are given everything for free
And accept it without gratitude
Their dog barks every morning
And continues through the nights
We hear the parents' constant rows
That always end in fights
Their broken stupid house alarm
With its piercing, awful clamour
That gradually shrieks into my brain
One day I'll fix it with a hammer
And whilst I'm in their garden
I'll shoot their mongrel dead
Then I'll take my target pistol
And put one in the mother's head
Then I'll continue through the family
As a vigilante blood-letter
Until they're all at my feet
And I'm feeling slightly better
Then I'll sneak around each room
As quiet as a mouse
Splashing petrol everywhere
And just burn down their house
Let this be a warning
To all scumbags far and near
This is a homewatch area
We don't want your type round here
To all who think I've gone too far
And have gone beyond the law
Bear in mind I'm watching you
I'm the one who lives next door......

Nightmare Scenario

Running from the bogey man
Look out he's got a knife
Down a hotel corridor
Hear screaming from the wife.

Turn to try to help her
Feet feel full of lead
Blood pouring from my open wounds
And dripping off my head.

Scenario suddenly changes
I'm on a motorway
With fast cars screaming past me
Drivers can't hear what I say.

Now on an escalator
Down into Hell's dark bowels
Hear scratching from behind me
And werewolves start their howls.

A mummy reaches for my sleeve
Emanating dust
A vampire tries to bite my neck
Filled with a wild blood lust.

Suddenly I'm on the stairs
And aged only three or four
Stare down at my broken toes
And blood upon the floor.

Then I'm on an alien world
And held down upon a rack
With scientific probes and wires
Projecting from my back.

I'm glued to a chair but hear her beg
For mercy – screaming "no!"
I look around to shout for help
But my words come out so slow.

I reach across to wake her up
But instead of her sleeping face
I notice to my horror
A corpse has filled her place.

I feel so sick, I can't escape
The dark shadows appear
I'm standing in a graveyard
An axe cuts off my ear.

The room spins fast around me
The walls ooze blood and gore
My muscles strain to bursting
I scream out loud "no more!"

The wife wakes up disgusted
And glares angrily at me
Saying "Next time before sleeping
Please don't have cheese for tea!"

Oh No! I've Killed the Wife!

Oh no! I've killed the wife! I said
I shot her after a row in bed
I've committed such an awful crime
I think I've gone too far this time.
Even though she ought to share the blame
She called me such an awful name!
Bound to happen in the end
I found out she had a secret friend
Some guy she was going to leave me for
Take my house and make me poor
So that was too much for me to take
I lay there for hours wide awake
And as our row went on all night
Bound to end in a vicious fight
Some harsh words so hastily said
No wonder that she'd end up dead!
The Police will soon be round for me
Won't be able to fob them off with tea
And however normally I might behave
They'd still notice a fresh dug grave…
So what can I do, what can I say,
To make those policeman go away?
I know, I'll hide her in the shed
And shovel soil over her head
And when the cops have a good look round

There'll be no disturbance in the ground
And if they ask where is your wife?
I'll say she's gone to watch East Fife
And if they return in a week or four
I'll say they're playing Stenhousemuir!
And for every month they demand a reason
Her absence is due to the football season!
And if they do investigate my shed
They still won't realise she's dead
For that earth I'll shape and well conceal
Each womanly curve from head to heel
With one bit protruding the way I like
Somewhere to be able to park my bike
And after a while when the mound does harden
I'll replant her in my vegetable garden
With various bits spread wide and loose
The girl at last will be of some use
And by the Spring there'll be new shoots
Instead of her bitter undyed roots
I'll sit there with my secret under ground
The peace and quiet newly found
And every home grown salad that I eat
Will have been fertilized at my feet
By one who never learned in life
A man with a gun beats a woman with a knife!

Political Correctness

There's nothing left to joke about
You've got to be "PC- wise"
Because if you say the wrong thing
You have to apologise
So no more jokes about Irishmen
Implying that they're thick
Or that Welshmen like to play with sheep
Or how Religion makes you sick
You can't make fun of any people
Who fit a common mould
Or laugh at a particular age group
Because that's calling people "old"
If you don't call Dwarves "vertically challenged"
You might just end up in court
Instead of like those good old days
When midgets were simply short
Foreigners, gays and cripples
Are no longer thought fair game
For our gentle British humour
That's earned us our terrible name
We can't criticize our neighbours
Or joke about terrorists crashing planes
We've lost our sense of gallows humour
In 911's remains
So if you're a foreign pregnant single parent
Who has one leg and one eye
I daren't say a thing about you
In case you moan, complain or cry
If you call me bitter and twisted
And think I've gone insane
You're no longer allowed to say that -
I'm just idiosyncratic in my brain
But nowadays it seems that non-correctness
Is really far too rare
When everyone looks so bloody miserable
- I know, I'm not allowed to swear -
It's a shame that similar standards
Don't occur in other places
And we don't get shown equal respect
By other Colours, Creeds and Races
So, if you're fat, bald, short or stupid
Or just someone's poor Mother-in-Law
Why don't you try to get a sense of humour
And learn just what laughing's for...

Read All About it!

Got a job as a newspaper headline writer
It ended so quickly I was bemused
When my boss said I drove him crazy
And left my readers upset and confused!

I couldn't understand his problem
Or his sense of indignation
As far as I was concerned
Nothing needed explanation!

"Dead body found in cemetery"
Was the first thing that made him frown
I don't make up the stories
I just put all the details down!

Next was the story of a man
Whose wife had been gone for years
I just mentioned their occupations
Saying *Magician's Assistant disappears!*

The wording of my next headline
 Was politically correct
All I said was *"a man stole a battery*
And the police charged the suspect!"

By now my editor was quite distraught
And his nerves he said were shattered
Just because I reported *"a chip shop fight*
And said two men got battered!"

He said he couldn't trust my words
Or sentences or syntax
After my report on a local fete
Where" *kids made delicious snacks!"*

I couldn't see the problem
It all made sense to me
Even when I wrote *"a stolen painting*
Was discovered by a tree!"

Where's the difficulty
In reading what I said
After I reported
"Man found safe under bed!"

When a psychic suffered an accident
I wasn't being mean
Just because I said *"his predicament*
Was rather unforeseen!"

And as for the army UXB story
Security I didn't breach
By simply stating the obvious
With *"Shell dug up on beach!"*

He said the list was endless
Then read out the other times
When all the things I put down
Was a list of all my crimes!

"Camouflaged vehicle missing
Schizophrenic tried suicide twice
One legged man runs shoe shop
And police ring caught in vice!"

"Policeman helped dog bite victim
Thieves steal burglar alarm
Volunteers strike for pay rises"
I wasn't doing any harm!

"Protestors march over illegal immigrants
Lack of brains hinders research
New vaccine may contain rabies
Tree thief gets the Birch!

Next March before April
Farmer outstanding in his field
6 out of 7 dwarves not happy"
All my headlines he revealed!

"Postman gets the sack
Museum curator seeks a date
Paper shop folds after two weeks
Fitness trainer loses weight!"

Now my boss has told me
One more bad headline and I'm gone
So I reported with much sadness
"Writer now signs on!"

Road Rage!

Get out of the way you stupid git!
You're far too old to drive
Move that heap of junk you fool
How d'you manage to stay alive?
You silly cow
Get in the right lane
Oh, look, another prat!
There's white van man
And captain slow
And some tool in a baseball hat!
All these idiots in my way
Whilst I'm trying to get to work
Where does it say in the Highway Code
You have to be such a jerk?
Now a motor cyclist
And then an ice cream man
Then some Polish lorry driver
And a stupid caravan!
All we need now is a funeral
Or the flaming RAC
Why does every idiot
Have to be right in front of me?
Now some little hatchback
Doing twenty mph at least
I overtake at speed to see
It's driven by a Priest!
Sunday drivers everywhere
To make me scream and shout
Is the local lunatic asylum
Having its annual day out?
What the hell are those sirens for?
And flashing lights of blue and red
Not another accident!
More delays here up ahead
I'm sick of these bad drivers
You see them more and more…
Yes, Officer, what's the problem?
What the hell did you stop *me* for?

Salford Boy

This is my story
Of John Cooper Clarke
During the punk years
Made his mark
Drugs and drink
Led to excesses
Failure followed by
Hard won successes
Loved his prose
Loved his rhymes
Loved his venom
Even his crimes
Loner with a past
Wildly artistic
Now he's just
Another statistic
One skinny step away
From the rehab door
Don't see his kind
Round here no more
The lad from Salford
Epitomised cool
Got me writing poetry
Staying in school
Spiky hair
Pointed toes
Best of all
Poisonous prose
No one safe
From his bitter style
Punks all loved him
Made them smile
Now they've long gone
They're all new men
Drinking bottled water
In bed by ten

Those of us left
Here to mourn
Another false prophet
Another false dawn
Gave us hope
And said Rebel!
Led us smiling punks
Straight to hell
Writing bad rhymes
On toilet walls
Till finally heeding
The usual calls
To conform and fit
In our comfort zones
Accept mediocre
Stultify our moans
No more great parties
In the park
Simmering rebellion
After dark
Few of us left
He's not forgotten
Like Sid and Nancy
And Johnny Rotten
Icons once
Had their time
We continue
The struggle to rhyme
1977
Is left in the past
Remember what he said
Die young, live fast
But for one brief moment
We felt that spark
Thanks to the greatest
John Cooper Clarke.

Saturday Night, Sunday Morning

Smoke a bit of weed
Wear a traffic cone
Drink a bit of lager
Get a little stoned
Fighting football rivals
Singing football songs
Drink a few more beers
Try to speak in tongues
Act like fascist bullies
Scratch a few nice cars
Light and throw some fireworks
Hit a few more bars
Drink a few more lagers
Following Curry and Rice
Chatting up the women
Feels like Paradise!
Scaring late night shoppers
Wave the football shirt
Confronting all the locals
Someone could get hurt
Have a spitting contest
Snort a little coke
Make a racist comment
Tell a dirty joke
Act like thugs and morons
Show you're real men
Outnumber your opponents
By eight or nine or ten
Getting in a taxi
When it stops get out and run
Avoid paying for the journey
That's really half the fun
Antagonise policemen
Drink another can
Scream for your solicitor
When thrown into the van
The end of the night's adventures
Spent in a sobering jail
Signing for the paperwork
That explains about the bail...

Wake up tired
Feel quite ill
Take another
Headache pill
Black coffee
Orange juice
Stomach heaves
Bowels loose
Headache pounds
Temples throb
Can't face breakfast
Lose my job
Tongue is furry
Throat is raw
Knees are scraped
Knuckles sore
Brain still aching
Banging head
Eyes are streaming
Burning red
Mystery injury
To my foot
Earlobe's ripped
Eyebrow's cut
Hair pulled out
Scalp is torn
Wish I was dead
Or never born
Clothes are ruined
One shoe lost
Wallet empty
Count the cost
Feel embarrassment
Feel the pain
Make the promise
Never again
See note from Policeman
Pinned to door
Monday, nine a.m.
Court Four!

Sex!

Just came back from my doctor's
And he gave me shocking news
He said "Your breathing's awful
And a lung you just might lose
But there's a drastic remedy
That I heard of, from the East
To radically improve your breathing
You must become a sexy beast!
Now tell your wife I recommend
Lots and lots of sex
It'll improve your lung capacity
And put two inches on your pecs!"
So when I got home a little later
I didn't really explain myself
I just jumped straight on my missus
Putting stuff upon a shelf...
When I came round two minutes later
I was nursing a fat lip
My nose was bent and bloody
And there were bruises on my hip.
She stood there looking at me
As I lay bleeding on the floor
And said "it's not your birthday
What d'you try and do that for?"
I said "We must be more spontaneous
When it comes to having relations
It'll do us both the world of good
And might save me serious operations!
She said "Don't be stupid
Sex isn't for the likes of us
I bet you made this whole thing up
As you came back on the bus.
Didn't the doctor give you pills
Or medicine or ointment?
If you want a leg over with me mate
You'd better make an appointment!
So while you lie there thinking
If there's even the remotest chance
You'd better bring me flowers and chocolates
And begin a little romance...
Cos you don't get something for nothing
So act like when you first knew me
Where's the wine and candles
As you try to charm and woo me?

A girl needs to feel special
Try to make me laugh, or flirt
Don't just grab me from behind
With your hand halfway up my skirt!"
Finally, after an hour's chat
We managed to agree
That if I helped more around the house
She'd find more time for me
So now I knew just what to do
To get my wife to play
I'd get the place all spick and span
Then she'd do things my way.
So I tidied up the front room
And emptied all the bins
I threw out all the pizza boxes
And all the lager tins
So once I'd scrubbed the bathroom
Bleached the toilet, cleaned the shower
She put on a really sexy dress
And went out for half an hour...
While she was out I dusted
Then vacuumed everywhere
I cleaned the kitchen till it gleamed
And sprayed freshener in the air
In fact the house was spotless
From the bottom to the top
I'd worked so diligently
With dusters, cloths and mop...
She came back a little later
With some Ann Summers underwear
But I was lay exhausted
Crashed out in a comfy chair.
So now I'm feeling better
The wife's opened up my eyes
Don't tire yourself out chasing girls
Just get some exercise!
And if you think that exercise
Isn't all that much fun
If you're sat around your filthy home
There's plenty housework to be done!
The point to my story
Finally makes sense in my head
Is that there's no reason to live longer
If your sex life's already dead!

She's a New Woman

Mavis could hardly believe it
All of her dreams had come true
When she matched all six balls on the lottery
She knew at once what she wanted to do.
Once the cheque was handed over to her
She was so happy she thought she might burst
But when they asked her to pose for the photos
She said "I'll have some repair work done first."
So she rang up the best plastic surgeon
And booked him for jobs lasting weeks
She had her boobs done, then some off her stomach
And all the fat sucked from her cheeks.
She got her feet done by an expert
Whilst another doctor worked on her eyes
When she finally emerged from the hospital
She would give her family and friends a surprise.
After new teeth and long hair extensions
And new nails from a glitzy nail bar
Proud Mavis stepped out into traffic
Then got hit by a fast moving car.
Unfortunately, for Mavis it was fatal
And although the driver got banned
Poor Mavis got sent straight to Heaven
Seeing God earlier than originally planned.
So the moral of this tale is a warning
To all who go under the knife
Remember, surgery may cost a small fortune
But it only lasts as long as one's life!
So when she saw God she was angry
And she yelled "Oi, God, that was sick!
I got all of this work done for nothing –
What a horribly cruel, rotten trick!"
So God, who was busy making thunder,
Turned to see what all the fuss was about
He looked at Saint Peter, then Mavis
And said "Sorry, my dear, did you shout?"
Mavis repeated her complaint to Saint Peter
Who spoke to God for a minute or two
He said "Sorry, Mavis, for all the confusion –
Neither one of us realised it was you!!!!"

Smoking is Bad for You

I was getting in my car today
And some bloke asked me for a light
But I was in a hurry so
I drove off into the night

When I reached the street corner
There to my surprise
Was that same fellow once again
With a strange look in his eyes

He looked a wee bit creepy
So I took off straight away
But he managed to keep up with me
As I shot down the highway

When I got up to thirty
The strange bloke was still there
He wasn't half moving bizarrely
And it gave me quite a scare

By the time the car reached forty
He was still there at my side
I wondered what would happen next
As we sped along our chilling ride

My foot pressed down that pedal
And when it reached the floor
The speedometer read sixty eight
But he stayed there by my door

So I increased up to eighty
With this maniac keeping pace
The wind distorted his features
As we held our scary race

By the time we reached a hundred
We were on the motorway
And he was banging on the glass
With a word or two to say

So that's when I did the unexpected
And stamped on the brakes so hard
And finally we shot off the motorway
Into a timber yard

I jumped out of my car at once
To confront the little creep
I looked all round the wood yard
Till I found him in a heap

His legs were pointing sideways
His arms were covered in blood
And his head was jammed into his neck
He didn't look too good.

I grabbed him by the collar
And my hands tightened even more
As I shouted in his face
"Just what did you do that for?"

He was quite apologetic
As he lay there on the floor
Saying "my jacket caught the handle
As you shut your driver's door!"

I said "that proves that smoking
Can be really bad for you"
But he replied "not really -
I only have an odd one or two."

Snow, snow, thick, thick snow.

In the wastes of frozen Antarctica
Over a hundred years ago
Sat Captain Scott, in a little tent
With his crew, knee deep in snow.

Said Captain Scott 'Now listen, chaps
Things are looking rather bleak
We're running out of rations
'cause we only catered for one week.

Now Amundsen and his lot
Are racing for the pole
Whilst five of us are stuck here
With just one solitary sausage roll.

We've got a pack of biscuits
I'd left them in my pack
I was sort of saving them
To munch on our way back.

But since we're pretty desperate
And you've been such a cracking crew
We'll open up these Hob Nobs
If someone rustles up a brew.

Now form a queue and have just one each
And take tiny little bites
These biccies may have to last us
For twenty or thirty nights.

If only we had thought to bring
At least double our supplies
We could be having beans on toast
Or steak and kidney pies.'

Bowers was first to whinge and moan
About their meals of just one course
He almost caused a mutiny when
He said "I could really eat a horse!

I wish Antarctica had an Asda
A Sainsbury's or Co-op
Then, if we needed anything
We'd just send Wilson to the shop.

Do you know what that swine Amundsen took?
Though it wasn't a bad idea
To have a doubly insulated modern tent
That he purchased from IKEA."

Then Evans stuck his head outside
And said "we really should get going"
Scott replied 'hang on a bit –
At least till it stops snowing.'

Eventually, in a tent so small
Captain Oates was first to feel the strain
Saying "Sorry, chaps, I've broken wind"
The others went insane.

Finally Scott had had enough
Of complaints and fear and doubt
That they'd never see the U.K. again
He thought 'Sod this, I'm going out!'

Now no-one ever visits the spot
Where Scott finally lost control
Or the remnants of that journey marked
By a frozen sausage roll.

Thank God!

No more discarded dirty underwear
No more bleached blonde hairs in the sink
No more half emptied pot noodle cartons
No more empty bottles of drink
We've seen the last of tights in the bathroom
We hear no more slamming doors
Now devoid of teenage temper tantrums
No more "that's mine and not yours"
It's the end of late night music
No more telly - midnight till three
No more cereals and milk going missing
No more of "what about me?"
It's the end to Mum's and Dad's taxis
It's the end to "can I have some cash?"
No more hairspray all over the mirrors
No more bins overflowing with trash
She's finally got her stuff all together
And decided to live with a mate
It's the end to coming home paralytic
And singing drunken songs until late
A lack of arguments of sister v sister
No more fights and coming home in tears
The house no longer rowdy but silent
The quietest that it's been for years
No more lipstick smears on the furniture
No mascara brushed against my white shirt
No nail polish dripped onto carpets
Or stilettos that track in the dirt
Finally, a house no longer untidy
No cigarette stubs dropped on the stairs
Or ashtrays for others to empty
Or food spilt down the sides of the chairs
No chocolate wrappers dropped for the cleaner
Or beans on toast left under the bed
No dizzy daughter in a Black Maria taxi
With an ice pack on the side of her head
So to my daughter's wonderful boyfriend
Some advice that I think you might lack
Please take real good care of my baby
But don't ever think of bringing her back!

The Truth

It's not you, it's me – I'm sorry
Something's changed within my heart
So I suppose I ought to tell you
Just how I think we've grown apart.

Remember in the old days
I enjoyed your quirky giggle
The way you ate and when in bed
The way you'd move and wriggle.

But now a long time later
And after every memorable date
I'm thinking lots of negatives
And realise so many things I hate.

The way I tolerated blithely
Your faults so irritating
And the bad habits I ignored so often
And how much you kept me waiting.

The times you were so nasty
And sarcastic to my friends
And the treatment of my family
How they'd prayed this union ends.

You killed off all my goldfish
And murdered my prize birds
And the manner of the dog's sad death
Still leaves me lost for words.

So pack your stuff, get out my sight
With your complaining and your moans
And that irritating speech impediment
I hate the way it drones.

I'm up to here with your snorting cough
And your horrible grating laugh
So take your rancid duvet covers
And your ring around my bath.

And whilst we're on the subject
Of the crap that you've brought here
You can shift your awful perfume
And shampoo that smells of beer.

No more will I have to tolerate
Your dirty sweat stained brother
Or hear that same old boring anecdote
About how your father met your mother.

Speaking of your parents
And their familiarity with disease
I admit I suspected all along
That they gave my poor cat fleas.

You emptied out my bank account
On things that were such a waste
I wouldn't have minded all that much
If you showed a modicum of taste.

And once you wrecked my home and garden
Then destroyed my vintage car
I couldn't stand you any more
You finally went too far.

So I'm going to say this to you
Please don't start to cry
I'll sum up our relationship
In just one word... GOODBYE!

Tummy Trouble

Our Janice was feeling quite poorly
And shook like she had jelly legs
I think it was something she'd eaten
Probably the bacon and eggs.
See, we'd stayed at this guest house in Blackpool
It was run by a really nice bloke
His wife, she did all the cleaning and cooking
His son did bugger all, except smoke.
Now the son I thought looked a bit shifty
And he gave our young Janice the eye
We noticed them touching hands over dinner
When he passed her the veal and ham pie.
Every moment she seemed to spend with him
Was like she wanted a ring on her hand
He kept taking her off for an ice cream
While the rest of us played on the sand.
Maybe it was all of the eating
She's not used to getting a lot
Up here you can get seafood portions
Supplied with a spoon, in a pot.
So one night at our holiday banquet
When she went for the oysters and trout
I could tell that he's watching our Janice
And I guessed what he's thinking about.
When he comes over all oily and greasy
With that look that can turn a girl's head
And he sees what she's got on her plate there
Then says "d'you fancy some sausage instead?"
So off they both go to the kitchen
And she's gone for the best part of an hour
When she comes back she's licking her fingers
And her dress is all covered in flour.
I don't like him, I tell the missus
Have you seen him? He's thin as a rake
He's certainly after our Janice
Next thing he'll be offering her cake.
So now that we're back home from Blackpool
I hope he's not planted his seed
Cause the last thing we need in this household
Is another hungry mouth hole to feed.
Finally Janice comes out with the answer
And there was us thinking she'd sinned
She'd been stuffing herself on his meatloaf
And the pains were just simply…trapped wind!

Two Sides

To maintain the universal balance
All things must possess equal parts
Like yin has yang and good has bad
Or diamonds have… spades, clubs and hearts.

Being kissed you might think is fantastic
To most people the idea sounds just great
But the bad side of a kiss situation
Is when the kisser is your prison cell mate.

Swimming in a warm sea is appealing
You could do that all day, until dark
But the image becomes rather scary
When you're the next likely meal for a shark.

A beautiful sunset's a favourite to many
But even this joy might be muted
If the end of this particular evening
Is this time when one gets executed.

It's nice to feel another's arms around you
And find yourself held really tight
Except if the holder's a mugger
And you're in a dark alley at night.

A soft pillow you would think of as cosy
In a warm bed would be a great place
But not if you're in an asylum
And an Indian's holding it over your face.

So the theory I'm trying to promote here
Which is proven many times every day
Is that for every possible silver lining
There's a dark cloud not too far away.

Viking Funeral

Don't put on black
Or wear a veil
Don't show a frown
Be deathly pale
Don't return
My library book
Or wear a dark
And solemn look
Don't gather the clans
Or ring my friends
Don't make a list
Where acquaintance ends
Don't weep or wail
Don't moan or cry
Don't stop all the clocks
Don't wave goodbye
Don't burn a longboat
Far out at sea
No Norseman's funeral
For the likes of me
Don't search for cash
Don't pawn my rings
Don't sell off all
My sentimental things
Don't shred my clothes
Or bin my shoes
Or donate those things
Charity shops can use
Don't cancel subscriptions
Of my magazines
Don't throw away
My favourite jeans
Don't burn my books
Don't sell my pets
Or put down my animals
At the vets
Don't say life gets lonely
As you get old
It's not swine flu
It's just a cold!

We Used to be Lovers

I saw you there beside the road
Heavy shopping in your hands
And remembered how you treated me
When I leapt to your commands
I saw the laugh lines on your face
And the wrinkles on your brow
The years have not been kind to you
You've paid beauty's price, and how!
I saw the two kids at your side
And heard their infant screaming
I saw your belly swelled again
And your skin no longer gleaming
I saw your hair has now grown grey
And there's dullness in your face
I saw your shoulders slumped in pain
How your eyes are an empty place
I saw that life has dragged you down
Then remembered what you did to me
I thought you looked so wretched
And so filled with misery
I saw your clothes so threadbare
And your shoes all cracked and worn
And like my heavy broken heart
Inside, all ripped and torn
I saw the heavy rain beat you down
And the large puddle at your feet
So I drove, spraying unmercifully
Now you know Revenge is sweet!

Psychopoetry

Puppy

I BOUGHT A LITTLE PUPPY
BUT NOW HE'S GONE TO HEAVEN
I THOUGHT HE WOULD BE WARMER
AT GAS MARK NUMBER SEVEN

Assistant

I ONCE WORKED AS A MAGICIAN'S ASSISTANT
AND WE CUT A WOMAN IN FOUR
THE TROUBLE WAS I DID IT LENGTHWAYS
AND USED MY DAD'S NEW CIRCULAR SAW

Circus

I ONCE TRIED FOR A JOB IN A CIRCUS
A KNIFE THROWER'S APPRENTICE I'D BE
BUT IT ALL WENT WRONG ONE THURSDAY
WHEN I PINNED A WOMAN TO SEAT FIFTY THREE

Ghost

I'M NOT THE LEAST BIT FRIGHTENED OF GHOSTS
REMEMBER WHAT THE NUMBER ONE RULE IS
SHOUT IF YOU'RE GRABBED BY THE BANSHEES
AND CRY IF YOU'RE GRABBED BY THE GHOULIES

Executed

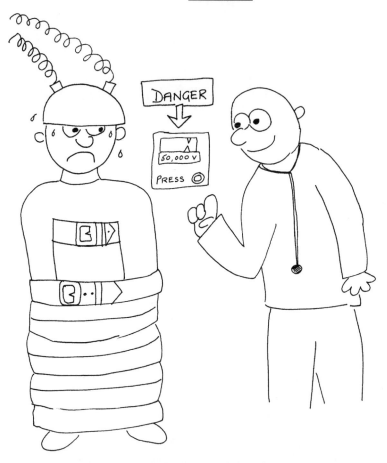

THEY JUST EXECUTED A MURDERER
A GOOD THING I'M SURE YOU'D AGREE
THAT WAS A LUCKY COINCIDENCE
HOW HE BORE SUCH A RESEMBLANCE TO ME

Inside

OF ALL THE PEOPLE INSIDE MY HEAD
I LIKE THE MURDERER THE MOST
HE MAKES LIFE VERY INTERESTING
SENDING BODY PARTS TO FRIENDS IN THE POST

People

PEOPLE DON'T UNDERSTAND ME
THEY SAY I'M A PSYCHOPATH RAVING
BUT MY DEFINITION OF THAT WORD
IS A MAN WHO LAYS CRAZY PAVING

Gorilla

I ONCE CAPTURED A GORILLA CALLED SIMBA
FOR THE ZOO – WHERE HE MADE PEOPLE CURIOUS
ONCE WE KEPT HIM APART FROM THE FEMALES
WILD? - I'D SAY HE WAS FURIOUS

Dad

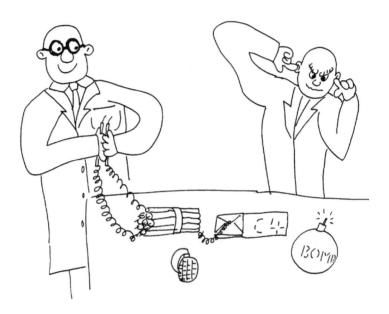

I'LL NEVER FORGET MY DAD'S LAST WORDS
THEY'RE SO POIGNANT NOW THAT HE'S GONE
HE SAID (HOLDING TWO WIRES TOGETHER)
"IT'S ALRIGHT, THE ELECTRIC'S NOT ON"

Holidays

I'M PACKING A BAG FOR MY HOLIDAYS
I'VE CHOSEN A REALLY NICE PLACE
THE FAMILY CAN COME FOR NO EXTRA CHARGE
IF I CAN GET THEM INSIDE THIS SUITCASE

Kidnappers

KIDNAPPERS ONCE CAPTURED MY CHILDREN
AND THE SUM THEY DEMANDED WAS LARGE
BUT AFTER A FORTNIGHT WITH THOSE KIDS
THEY SENT THEM ALL BACK FREE OF CHARGE

Adore

I ADORE YOUR BODY MY DARLING
MY LOVE FOR YOU GROWS AND GROWS
FROM WHAT'S LEFT OF THE HAIR ON YOUR HEAD
TO THE TAG ON YOUR PRETTY LITTLE TOES

Rebels

FATHER FOUGHT ALONGSIDE THE REBELS
MOTHER SEWED THE SHROUDS FOR THE DEAD
MY BROTHER WAS THE HEAD OF THE RESISTANCE
MY JOB WAS BUTTERING THE BREAD

Nightmare

I'M HAVING THAT RECURRING NIGHTMARE
WHERE THE MANIAC CHOPS OFF MY HEAD
I DON'T DO ALL THAT MUCH SWEATING
BUT MAKE A HELL OF A MESS IN MY BED

Clown

I GOT A LIFT HOME FROM A CLOWN ONCE
THE SMOKE FROM HIS CAR MADE ME COUGH
WE ONLY MANAGED TWENTY FIVE YARDS
WHEN THE ROOF AND BOTH DOORS JUST FELL OFF

Sneaky

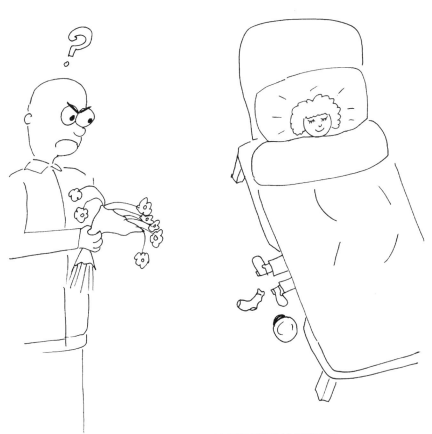

I SNEAKED UP ON MY WIFE THIS MORNING
I KISSED THE BACK OF HER NECK TO HER KNEES
BUT SHE JUST TURNED AND SAID, SMILING
"JUST TWO PINTS TODAY, MILKMAN, PLEASE"

Business

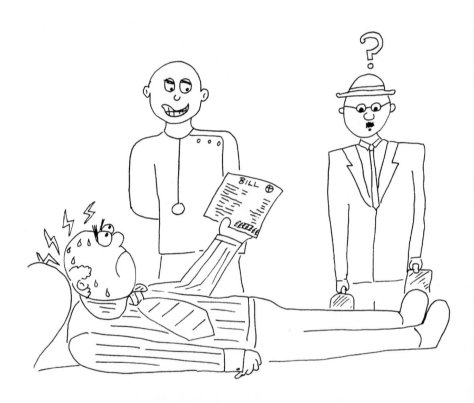

A BUSINESSMAN, DYING, CALLED HIS DOCTOR
HAVING SEVERE SHOOTING PAINS IN HIS HEAD
BUT WHEN HE RECEIVED THE MEDICAL BILL
HE CRIED OUT FOR HIS ACCOUNTANT INSTEAD

Michelangelo

MICHELANGELO – UPSIDE DOWN ON A SCAFFOLD
SAID "POPE JOHN PAUL IS VERY UNFEELING
I PAINT THE SISTENE CHAPEL FOR SEVEN YEARS
NOW HE WANTS A SECOND COAT ON THE CEILING"

Elephant

LAST NIGHT I SHOT AN ELEPHANT
IN MY PYJAMAS – AFTER A VERY LONG CHASE
THE QUESTION I WANT TO ASK IS....
WHY'S HE WEARING THEM IN THE FIRST PLACE?

Moaning

I'M MAKING A VERY STRANGE MOANING SOUND
YOU COULD SAY I'M STARTING TO PANIC
I DON'T LIKE THE LOOK OF THAT ICEBERG
FROM HERE ON THE S.S. TITANIC

<u>Stanley</u>

STANLEY MATTHEWS AT EIGHTY FIVE
COULD STILL LEAVE HIS NURSES IN AWE
WITH SWERVES DOWN ALL THE HOSPITAL WINGS
AND DRIBBLES ALL OVER THE FLOOR

Poor

BEING POOR MEANT NO MONEY FOR LAXATIVES
SO WE SPENT MANY A LONG HOUR IN THE LOO
TILL MY DAD SAT US DOWN ON THE POTTY
AND READ US ALL A GHOST STORY OR TWO

Yacht

THE LAST ROUND THE WORLD YACHT RACE
WAS WON BY OLD FERGUS O'CONNOR
HE DIDN'T STOP TO COLLECT HIS TROPHY
BUT SAILED OFF ON A QUICK LAP OF HONOUR

Demons

DEMONS AND ANGELS ARE BATTLING
OUR SPIRITUAL FUTURES THEIR GOALS
IS IT WORTH A FIGHT BETWEEN GOOD AND EVIL
FOR THE SAKE OF A BUNCH OF OUR SOULS?

Test

RECRUITED IN AN M.I.5. SPY TEST
THEY SAID "SHOOT YOUR WIFE" FOR A DARE
BUT SOMEBODY PUT BLANKS IN THE PISTOL
SO I CLUBBED HER TO DEATH WITH A CHAIR

S & M

A MASOCHIST AND A SADIST SAT TOGETHER
BOTH OF THEM ARE FEELING QUITE LOW
SO THE MASOCHIST JUMPS UP AND SAYS HURT ME
BUT THE SADIST JUST SMILES AND SAYS NO

Wonder Woman

I ONCE SAW WONDER WOMAN NAKED
SHE'S MY FAVOURITE SEXUAL DREAM
SO I JUMPED ON HER WITHOUT WARNING
THEN HEARD MISTER INVISIBLE SCREAM

Zombie

A ZOMBIE CRAWLED OUT OF THE GRAVEYARD
AND WENT INTO THE PUB FOR A BEER
WHEN THE BARMAN SAID "YOU WANT A LAGER?"
THE ZOMBIE SAID "NO THANKS, I'VE ONE EAR"

Mary

MARY HAD A LITTLE LAMB
SHE WENT AND CALLED IT HILDA
IT WASN'T MUCH PROTECTION
WHEN SOMEBODY WENT AND KILLED HER

Bargain

I'M ALWAYS ON THE LOOKOUT FOR BARGAINS
IF I MISS ONE I FEEL RATHER SORRY
LIKE WHEN I MET THE WIFE AT AN AUCTION
SHE JUST FELL OFF THE BACK OF A LORRY

Hands

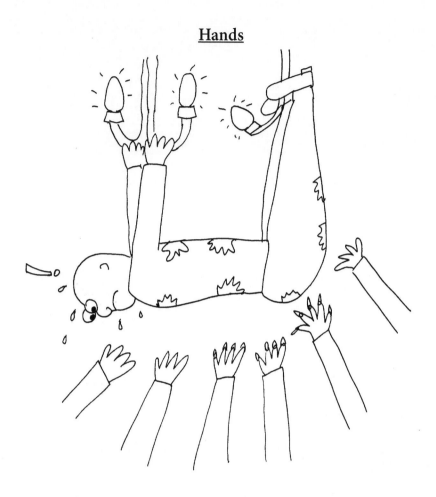

HANDS GRASPING AT YOUR VITAL PARTS
SKIN TORN AND BLEEDING FROM NAILS
AN HORRIFIC VISION OF HELL?
NO – THE START OF THE JANUARY SALES

Tea

HAD MY PARENTS FOR TEA
AND ALSO MY AUNTIE
THEY WENT WELL WITH SOME FAVA BEANS
WASHED DOWN WITH CHIANTI

Zoo

ALL ZOO KEEPERS ARE NERVOUS ROUND TIGERS
OUR LAST CHAP WE HAD TO REPLACE
HE ONLY WENT IN THE CAGE DURING LUNCHTIME
NOW THE TIGER'S GOT HIS SMILE ON ITS FACE

Cannibals

IF YOU EVER GET CAUGHT BY THE CANNIBALS
AND OUT COME THEIR KNIVES FORKS AND PLATES
JUST TELL THEM YOUR BODY'S UNHEALTHY
AND TOO HIGH IN POLYUNSATURATES

Houdini

I'M EVER SO SORRY MISTER HOUDINI
AS YOU WERE DROPPED IN THE THAMES IN A BOX
THERE'S ONE THING I NEGLECTED TO MENTION
I'M STILL HOLDING YOUR KEYS TO THE LOCKS

Frankenstein

FRANKENSTEIN MADE A MONSTER FROM CORPSES
AND ROBBING FRESH GRAVES IN THE NIGHT
THE LEGS WERE FROM TWO DIFFERENT PEOPLE
I THINK YOURS WAS THE ONE ON THE RIGHT

A THISTLEDOME PRODUCTION

Printed in Great Britain
by Amazon.co.uk, Ltd.,
Marston Gate.